I0158648

Anthony Kearney

LIFE BEGINS AT
SIXTY

How to jump off the retirement
scrapheap and start living

Anthony Kearney

LIFE BEGINS AT
SIXTY

How to jump off the retirement
scrapheap and start living

MEMOIRS

Cirencester

Mereo Books

1A The Wool Market Dyer Street Cirencester Gloucestershire GL7 2PR
An imprint of Memoirs Publishing www.mereobooks.com

Life begins at Sixty: 978-1-86151-520-9

First published in Great Britain in 2015
by Mereo Books, an imprint of Memoirs Publishing

Copyright ©2016

Anthony Kearney has asserted his right under the Copyright Designs and Patents
A CIP catalogue record for this book is available from the British Library.

This book is sold subject to the condition that it shall not by way of trade or otherwise be lent,
resold, hired out or otherwise circulated without the publisher's prior consent in any form of
binding or cover, other than that in which it is published and without a similar condition,
including this condition being imposed on the subsequent purchaser.

The address for Memoirs Publishing Group Limited can be found at www.memoirspublishing.com

The Memoirs Publishing Group Ltd Reg. No. 7834348

The Memoirs Publishing Group supports both The Forest Stewardship Council® (FSC®) and the
PEFC® leading international forest-certification organisations. Our books carrying both the FSC
label and the PEFC® and are printed on FSC®-certified paper. FSC® is the only
forest-certification scheme supported by the leading environmental organisations including
Greenpeace. Our paper procurement policy can be found at
www.memoirspublishing.com/environment

Typeset in 11/17pt Century Schoolbook
by Wiltshire Associates Publisher Services Ltd. Printed and bound in Great Britain by
Printondemand-Worldwide, Peterborough PE2 6XD

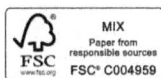

MIX
Paper from
responsible sources
FSC
www.fsc.org FSC® C004959

PEFC
PEFC/16-33-415

My thanks to all those who made this book possible: Jenny, Ingela, Badger and many others who gave me feedback on my unique ideas.

Artwork by Karin Söder from Lycksele, Sweden.

Also by Anthony Kearney:

The Pursuit of Happiness

(Mereo, 2016)

contents

Introduction

This is my second book on happiness. The first, "The Pursuit of Happiness", was written for members of the public of any age. This book is intended for those people who are approaching retirement age and view their future with some doubt, or even dread. You are, after all going to be viewed by your government and society as 'past your use-by date'. This is especially so of men, but this book is aimed at those men and women who chose a working life path in a career.

In my first book I showed you how to choose a happiness-giving life path after discovering what sort of person you were.

Some of the words and phrases you may find difficult to understand, as they represent new ideas. I have therefore included a short list of definition of phrases and words to launch you with confidence into this book.

Like the first book, this is a 'self-help' book.

Definitions

Reality Differential Factors are the differences in inputs between the present real world and a more perfect past, future or imaginary world.

Zone of Equanimity (ZOE) is the zone in which we exist. It has four Domains (referred to as 'Selves'), each of which can contribute to the state of the Zone and interact with the external world.

Low Reality Differential Factors (low RDFs) - Think of these as 'good' things leading to elation, or 'positive inputs'.

High Reality Differential Factors (high RDFs) - Think of these as 'bad' things leading to depression, or 'negative inputs'.

Depression - a state of more high RDFs than low RDFs, giving you a Zone of Equanimity centred in the depression side of the Zone.

Elation - a state of more low RDFs than high RDFs, giving you a Zone of Equanimity centred on the elation side of the Zone.

Reality Differential Factor Analysis (RDA or RDF analysis) - Think of this as an assessment of you as a person which is designed to demonstrate how balanced or unbalanced your life is.

Reality Analysis (RA) - A possible basis for therapy.

1
The Awakening

When I was a boy I would often hear grizzly, wrinkled-faced men talking about when life began. "Life begins at 40", they would say with a nod and a wink to each other. As a boy I found this disconcerting, as it meant my life had not yet begun and that I had to wait some 26 years before it would. This troubled me for many years after, because it seemed as if I was playing with time waiting for the day when my life began. I recall thinking that the whole notion was one put about by old men to justify their lives after 40.

This notion was strengthened when I awoke one day to find that I was legally a man. I had reached 21 and at the stroke of midnight, at the commencement of that notable day things would somehow be different, but they were not. Apart from a few people saying "Happy birthday!" and "Are you going out for a beer?" nothing changed. I suppose I became a little more 'macho' and pointed out to various youngsters that they had a way to go before they had the full rights and privileges that age brings. But this was only banter, as we all knew that nothing would really change.

When I eventually reached 40 I had begun to realise that at that age disillusionment had crept into my view of life. Was this what it was all about, or had I missed something? I felt that I must have missed something, so in an effort to find what it was I took my ancient boat *Rimudo* to the Mediterranean via Switzerland. I could have taken the chicken run via the Seine and Paris, and the Rhône and Saône rivers and canal system to Marseilles. I could have gone via the Bay of Biscay, but as the boat was held together with putty and bits of glass fibre I felt it would fall apart, thus defeating the object. I had two friends with me Juliet and Mick, neither of whom seemed to be aware that the trip was somehow not to be included in their lives, as they had 19 years to go before reaching 40, and their lives were therefore in some way in embryo.

Their job was to raise funds for the travel costs to enable me to start the life which would now happen because I was 40. This they did by playing the clarinet and guitar. Despite my noble position in the age scale I found that our enjoyments were the same as were our trials and tribulations. The age difference did not appear to affect our life experiences.

After a year in the Mediterranean sun I returned to England, only to find that despite my life now really beginning it did not seem any different to me from before, and I forgot the whole idea of life beginning at 40 and wrote it off as something people said to the young in order that they did not rebel against society, which would reward them at 40.

Since those days in the 1980s life has progressed, but I would not say that it started at any point. More likely I had accepted what it appeared to be and copied everyone else in obtaining its benefits. From the early 80s I studied psychology and psychotherapy, but the answers could not be found in the framework of knowledge, despite this knowledge being comprehensive. It was towards the middle of the 90s that a new theory of the person began to develop, (this appears in my book *The Pursuit of Happiness*) and it was from this theory that I started to make sense of what 'Life begins at 40' meant. But I was not happy with my conclusions, as they seemed to contradict the evidence all around me from people's lives.

It appeared that 40 was the age at which one started to condition oneself that retirement was approaching, as was the end of one's 'useful' life. Far from life beginning at 40, I started to assess what they had gained to sustain them through 'old age', as 60 was deemed to be. This in effect focused my mind onto future needs up to the dying age. From my boyhood days I had been told that this was threescore years and ten and had always been so. It was in the Bible, so it must be true. Lo, all around me people are dying between 60 and 80 in great numbers, so that was further proof that 40 was the middle of life, and that life beginning at 40 was a preparation for that goal in life, of death.

Two things changed my view of this opinion, one was a court case and the other was a scientific paper. The court case involved a man of 60 and two women who were causing a public disturbance over the man. The judge concluded that they should sort things out between themselves and not be unseemly, at their age. The man received a strange response from the judge, who expressed the view that at his age the defendant should have got things sorted out with his female friends. The judge then said that the man who had said life began at 40 was 20 years out. This amused the press, which printed details of the case. I did not really think much about the case for the next few weeks as I was working on my theory, but I was pleasantly surprised when an article appeared in the press written by a scientist and saying that humans should live to 120!

Life begins at 60!

Then one day it struck me: 40 was the social or societal middle age, and was linked to economic worth. Sixty was the true age of middle age and linked to natural death, assuming you were not diseased or had abused yourself. In the societal setting such activities as sitting, watching TV, over-indulging in food or drink and a general sedentary lifestyle were expected from 60. Indeed since the vast population of the Western World subscribes to the idea that 60 is old, and civil servants and pension fund administrators rub their hands as they see the lifestyle of their pensioners precipitating an early death.

Very few 60-year-olds actually start new lives, because the majority have such a huge psychological hurdle of opinion to negotiate. Usually they drift with the tide of requirements in their home or nursing home. This is especially true of men, who are less socially adapted to domestic routines than women. We are told that women have a 'social gene' which automatically predisposes them to home organisation. Women still live longer than men, so if men want to extend their lives towards 120 it is imperative that they discover enough about themselves to really begin life at 60.

To do this it is going to be necessary to briefly outline Differential Theory as it affects men and the structure of the person. Differential Theory deals with how each person is structured. Personality Theory deals with how the structure creates the person. Each of us is as you know one person, but what you may not know is how you can be changed by your own efforts. Change is almost certainly a need once you are 60. Failure to change will ensure that you will die at the age socially decided by yourself and your family. Illness will assist in this process, as will a social interpretation of what 'old' people should do with themselves.

2

Our Selves

We exist in a zone of equanimity which is wide and adaptable when we are young, and narrows and is less responsive to 'inputs' as we grow older. Older people are less responsive because the stimulus is usually something they have experienced before. Therefore one key to living to an old age is new experiences.

The zone of equanimity (ZOE) starts to settle into its design style from an early age. The ZOE responds to 'good' things called Low Reality Differential Factor Inputs and to 'bad' things called High Reality

Differential Factor Inputs. The ZOE needs both RDFs to ensure that it undulates and is actively attempting to maintain a state of equanimity. This state we might call Happiness.

If the zone experiences only 'good' things, then for it to respond, these 'good' things must continuously be increased in intensity. This is a typical case for a performing artist or someone getting the habit of drug-taking. These constant 'good' things move the whole zone towards elation.

It is important that the zone does not reach the limit of its capacity, either in 'good' things or 'bad' things. If the zone experiences 'bad' things then overloading can result in depression as the zone moves into the side of depression. It is important to receive inputs of 'bad' RDFs to counter 'good' RDFs, but none of these inputs should move the zone permanently. A positive input moves the zone towards elation. A negative input moves the zone towards depression.

Now the ZOE has the simple task of gaining low RDFs to create a state we might call happiness. Low and high RDFs are usually of a transitory nature and the zone is inconsistent in its response to any stimulus. The zone response is dependent on what has gone before. For instance, something nice followed by something nice will cause the zone to respond differently to something unpleasant followed by something nice.

Probably all creatures, and certainly mammals, have a zone of equanimity. It will probably be structured similarly to humans but with very noticeable differences: one or two domains are missing. A domain is an area of ZOE. With humans there are four domains, and each has the ability to stand alone and control the position of the zone towards elation or depression. Control of the zone by one domain is very unusual, and for most people an impossibility.

The first domain is the Biological Domain. This is the domain which is involved in all basic physical functions, desires and needs of the body. Within this domain are the drives to satisfy these needs. This domain even has its own egoistic thinking and language, which is often highlighted by phrases starting with 'Give me', 'I want'. This is the domain which seeks to have its demands satisfied as a child. The way an adult responds will modify, or fail to modify, the child's behaviour in order for it to gain maximum low RDFs. Naturally at a young age a child will have no idea about controlling gratification and you will have seen an over-indulged child controlling the adults. You would say they have spoilt the child. Such children and their parents are ripe candidates for therapists specializing in forms of behavioural therapy.

The Biological Domain is the structure for the first of the selves. A biological self climbing a mountain on his own is functioning properly. He has no need to consider his three other selves, but as you will see they will appear and the appropriate domain will gain low and high RDFs.

A biological child – poor spoilt boy

The second of our domains to structure the ZOE is the Social Domain. This is the one which causes so many problems. This domain has to be educated. If it is not educated then it can be a cause of dissonance and disharmony between the two domains adjacent. This

domain enables you to gain pleasure from entertaining friends at a perfectly prepared dinner with candles, with the correct wine, sparkling glasses, perfect presentation of food and immaculate table linen. Such a meal gives immense low RDFs, but if something goes wrong then high RDFs will possibly precipitate a spoilt evening followed by a row, leading to high RDFs in other domains. Breeding, good manners, culture, social behaviour and treatment of others are the province of this domain. Whilst the biological domain response to someone making a pass at your wife would give you low RDFs as you punched him, the social repercussions the social domain will suffer would give your ZOE no real advantage. It may even leave you in a temporary state of depressive thought.

Biology at work

The social self is the one which uses a complex society to its advantage in order to gain low RDFs. A socially inadequate self can find that the inability to `fit in' with society causes high RDFs, which causes a depressed state. Such a depressed social self may resort to other domains to move the ZOE to a more equable state nearer to the elation side. Without a proper understanding of the social needs of the self, therapy is lost on the individual. He will take the easiest route to bring his ZOE towards elation. He calls on his biological self for help and then may move into drugs, alcohol, robbery, mugging, destruction, self-mutilation of the self which cannot fit in and over-eating. The list is probably not endless, but you get the idea. You have two selves which work independently of each other but both have the same psychological goal: low RDFs.

The third self is the cognitive self. This is developed from the cognitive domain, which is our factual and intellectual self. This domain gains low RDFs in planning and designing the structure of a house. It is the domain which men use when they retire from work and immediately start to spend all their time working out the house finances, working late at night and doing voluntary work of a similar nature to their past employment. The domain desperate to maintain low RDFs forces the self to work harder than it needs to gain low RDFs. All the domain understands is that the daily opportunities to gain low RDFs from say being a doctor, dentist, accountant, nurse or teacher have formally ended, and it forces the self to grasp at anything that will satisfy its desire. Eventually, of course the work does dry up and the ZOE receives insufficient stimulus

to keep it wide, so it narrows and ceases to respond to stimulation.

Freedom

As the selves within the zone cease to undulate by not acknowledging opportunities for ZOE inputs, so the individual starts to die. To the rescue of the cognitive self will come the biological and social self and for a while, holidays, new company and physical stimulations will keep the ZOE from depression, but unless a cognitive rescue package can be assembled, the self will be a drag on the ZOE and create a sense of loss. Loss as you know leads to depression. Of course the other two selves can experience loss on ceasing work.

The final domain to consider is the Psyche Domain. This is best imagined as the Spiritual Domain. For humans, stimulation of this domain and the receiving of low RDFs are fundamentally to wellbeing. The domain needs feeding rather than it has demands. It needs to appreciate the wonder of the sunset from a mountain top. It needs to be able to gain low RDFs from seeing the smiling face of a child on being greeted after a walk in the park. It needs to be able to contemplate the universe, the stars and the moon. It needs to be swept along by beautiful music.

The Psyche Shock

The psyche self is the one which is able to give away all its possessions just because it had little need for them and someone else did. The psyche self will give away all of a lottery win to charity or the 'needy' without consideration of the needs of the other three selves. The psyche self gains low RDFs from good work such as helping out at summer fetes, running an old people's voluntary club or just fishing by a river, contemplating the water and pond life. Catching a fish is an excuse to contemplate nature.

So you as a person are made up of four selves, each intent on gaining low RDFs for the ZOE. The sort of person you are depends on the interaction of these selves and was set in basic form before you became an adult. The opportunity to improve cognitively by going to university, such as the Open University, or by developing socially by entering a caring profession will add their values to the person. Such a compromise of selves is the average person.

You may have seen people with only two or three selves contributing to the person, for instance the teenager who has been in intensive care since birth and expects to die soon. Their biological self contributes little to their person. The inadequate social self is often seen in prisons, when the biological self has been allowed to take over in a social setting. The cognitive selves are seen most noticeably in court rooms and universities and are frequently devoid of any other selves when engaged in work. Finally, the psyche self expresses itself in the opera chorus, the church or nunnery. Their world is their life.

Among this group who gain so much from music are the opera singers. Few indeed are able to satisfy their psyches' needs once their voices have reached a peak and show signs of distress. Some are able to enter the conducting arena or the teaching of master classes, but for many their only chance of psyche stimulation is by observational involvement with someone younger. In the field of ballet, for example, choreography is a valid substitute for being a principal dancer.

So you say, "What about me?" When you are around 50 you need to look at your person and attempt to assess what each of your selves is getting from life. Then you need to work out how those selves can gain the low RDFs they are denied. You then need to work out what high and low RDFs will go when you cease work.

Finally a long-term plan needs to be put in motion so

that you can begin life at 60. This is not an easy exercise, especially since probably no one will be around to analyse you and present a zone of equanimity chart showing what state your zone is in and what low and high RDFs are missing. Fortunately an idea of what to do is outlined in my book on Happiness. This may be of help. Ideally you need someone to enlighten you. For this reason someone who will guide you to a successful start in life at 60 should not be someone who thinks you have a problem, ie the average therapist. However, since the issues involved are essentially psychological, it is likely that people in the field of therapy will take up the challenge of a new approach to guiding and helping people. But, beware, as RD analysis is not in itself a therapy, it does not mean that someone will not claim to be an RD therapist. Only those properly qualified in psychology will be able to give you a proper perspective of your person.

So, before you retire you need to assess your life and discover which of your selves has been dominant. That is almost certainly the one which will miss employment, but not necessarily so. My dominant self has always been my biological self and I always found the demands of employment a source of disharmony, principally because my free time was always prejudiced by the needs of the job. For most people the demands of the biological self are usually met in food prepared by the wife, sex with the wife and exhaustion from the children. My biological self had sporting aspirations, so it required more time than was available.

Enough about me. A new life is about dramatic change and ensuring that your ZOE gains inputs from all domains. So, let us look at reality from the standpoint of someone retiring and approaching the day the firm, or the office or fellow workers, prepare for the farewell occasion. This is the point when shock sets in.

3
Retirement

I am going to give you a hypothetical job type so that you can get some feel for how Reality Differential Theory works. I want you to imagine that you are retiring from an office job; perhaps in local government, a bank or building society, an accountancy firm etc. The actual job is not important; what is important is that they have all been using your social self with maybe a little help from your cognitive self. You have fitted into a social structure for the purpose of earning money.

Every evening your social self wanted peace, your

cognitive self wanted a new challenge and your other two selves wanted stimulation. Invariably you were disappointed and settled into a routine where your social self was not stressed. This usually meant that on arriving home the last thing you wanted was all the woes of your family. Frequently the escape from this social self overload of usually high RDFs was the pub, sports club or some means of switching off from the world. Fortunately you probably have a TV and so you and the rest of the family could switch off from the real world altogether.

So, as a middle manager in your firm you are prepared for a good send-off. Food and drink have been arranged and one of the directors from upstairs is coming down to make a presentation. The party starts and everyone seems immensely happy; well, everything is free. You get a little tipsy and relaxed. At a suitable point in the proceedings you are presented with your going-away gifts. The staff have bought you some drink and gardening tools for a window box. As you neither have a garden nor a window box in your apartment you look a little nonplussed. Then, "Silence everyone. The

MD would like to say a few words." The few words are said, the company presentation made, which is so often a clock, and the MD tells everyone to carry on. He takes you aside and gives you a brown envelope containing part of the pension lump sum and tells you that everything is in hand for your pension payments. You cannot stand the man, but he offers you part-time work after 'you have settled into retirement' and asks you to give the new office manager a ring in a few weeks. He suggests you leave now in order for everyone to say goodbye.

This is all done remarkably quickly and you soon find yourself on a cold windy pavement waving a taxi down. The drive home is a strange affair. Normally you go by car, but you knew you would not be able to drive. So for the first time in years you can think about your day.

Overriding all thoughts is the multitude of goodbyes. A sense of isolation and loneliness pervades you as you realise the whole building is full of people enjoying your loss. Their lives are now about to be changed for the better as everyone moves up the ladder in the company structure. Tomorrow, for them, new horizons will be opened up, but what of your horizon? What do you see ahead? What do you do tomorrow?

There are two scenarios. The first is that you become a potterer. You do all those jobs you have been meaning to do for the last 30 years but did not because you did not know how, or you were too tired from the weekly work. You seek odd jobs in the field of your work, but quickly find that the technology is leaving you behind. You become a wife follower; she shops, you follow, she takes the dog out, you follow. Your interest in life starts to revolve around your home and memories of past achievements. Oddly, new possible achievements cease to interest you, and like your dog you live from meal to meal and from day to day.

What is happening is that your ZOE is narrowing and ceasing to be affected by high or low RDFs. You are starting to die. One of your selves, probably the biological, will realise that life is 'killing you' and you become an irritable 'old' man. Like a child you then gain low RDFs from being 'naughty'. The alternative is that you become remarkably placid and talk to all manner of people. Your social self is attempting a comeback. When people are not around, your social self talks to your other selves. This is an area of harmony and often you prefer talking on your own than to the other old people you meet. The domains will dream up all sorts of things for your Selves to do for low RDFs, but sadly without a projected structure of life, it is like a man being given a rope simply because he is standing at the bottom of a mountain. The second scenario is what this book is all about.

If you are immensely lucky, by the time you are 60 you will be itching to begin life. Your preparation will have begun five to ten years earlier. Your company will have reduced your working week by one day in order for you to follow new interests. You have been sensible and studied what was not necessarily available at school, college or university. You choose to study those fields which will force you to change environments, meet new people and give you a sense of wonder. Such fields include archaeology, geology and ornithology. These fields give each domain an input. There are many others.

You may of course decide to pander to the needs of

your biological domain and prepare for adventure. Such an adventure might be learning to climb and giving as your goal the ascent of Everest, or sailing around the world or changing your wife for another. Each adventure has its own biological self challenge, and a great deal of preparation and ground work needs to be done first. For sailing the challenge is fairly simple, with you getting fit and learning new skills. However, you should beware. An adventure can, if not handled right, become the last action of a dying man. There must be life after the adventure, and this should be worked on before and after the challenge. Every challenge has its financial costs, and what started as a climb of Everest might eventually be a long trek over a range of smaller mountains in the company of others. The sailing trip might likewise be shorter or different simply because of crippling costs.

These changes you can accommodate, and they will still give you an adventure. These are 'launch pad' adventures and you will return a different person, at which point your wife might walk out or you might look for another. The effect of the launch pad is to widen your

ZOE, which has over the period of a few weeks been subjected to an immense number of high and low RDFs. Whatever the reason, it is not uncommon to change partners on retirement.

4

Wives, Mistresses, Lovers & Husbands

The common feature that mistresses and lovers have is that they are usually younger than their partners. Women beyond child-bearing age who sport a lover on their arm gain high numbers of low RDFs for their social self. Their biological self is hormonally boosted by an increase in sexual activity with a more stimulating partner. It too gains low RDFs. In Freudian terms, the women are perverts since they cannot have children. In

Reality Differential Theory they are perfectly normal, since they are only gaining RDFs.

What is surprising is that some of these women stay with one lover, when in fact it is normal for them to want a series of lovers to enrich their personal gene pool, which is what many young women do. The only explanation is that the social self is satisfied and together with the cognitive self had made it quite plain to the biological self that the object of many low RDFs has been achieved. It would be ZOE unbalancing if they took another lover simply because of the normal drive the biological self has for multiple partners. Its effort for the best genes for her offspring is way past her use-by date and therefore a waste of time. In other words "Biological self, baby, recognize that you are too old. Be happy with what you have!"

Ignoring the pressures of the cognitive and the social domains can lead to a new psychological/physical 'illness', sexaholism. In RDF terms the control of the person by the biological self's out-of-date drives represents a dangerous state for the ZOE (a reminder, Zone of Happiness) and the life of the individual.

A new wife

Hope he doesn't want sex!

Such a dilemma does not face the young lover. However, you are not going to be a young lover. You might at best be a 'toy boy' for some rich 80-year-old widow. Now she would gain all the advantages mentioned above and the added advantage that her toy boy would not run off at such a speed that she could not catch him. The feature common to rich old men and rich old women is that they have the power. They can always bring a younger partner back to their arms with diamonds, yachts, cars and expensive presents. So before you commit yourself to a woman, let me remind you what the main issue is.

Should you have an adventure with a new partner? An adventure is an occupation, event or lifestyle where there are a limited number of predictable situations, but many more unpredictable ones; it has a time limit. A new woman represents many unpredictables. That is the main issue.

The next is, what sort of relationship are you seeking for this adventure? You have a choice, husband or 'lover'. The question is not as simple as you might think, and neither is the answer. The lover is a biological self relationship, even though you might think the world of the lady and adore being in her company in a social context. She might even have similar cognitive interests as you and be very good company. However, once the biological self is satisfied with its gains, it then seeks other interests. Some men and women make the mistake that they think their biological relationship should have to be honoured with marriage, and the additional commitment makes the normal biological interest stage last for longer than it was meant to. Additionally, society and family increasingly make what should have been a short-term commitment into something that appears 'forever'. Children leaving home or the retirement of one or both parties is a typical time to call it a day, or take on a lover or mistress.

Biological Adventures

A wife is totally different from a mistress, and a husband is likewise different from a lover. Marriage is a social self commitment. Unlike the lover and mistress, the other selves are engaged. Many of the most stable marriages are only that way because the social selves of both parties realise what they are up to. Since the object of the social self is to do the best it can to make the relationship pleasant, as well as long lasting, both parties will draw on the other three to help sustain the relationship.

Establishment people who have much to lose by way of friends, relations and their place in society maintain the marriage status until death. In truth, as both partners have been having affairs but get on well together, there is really no cause to separate. One is constantly amazed to see famous people in court over alleged dealings with 'other women' and occasionally other men, with their wives hanging on their arm posing as the proud, dutiful wife. Mind you, she knows, and so does the world, that her husband can still perform in bed. That is an immense boost to the social self. After all, many women would love to have a husband who was still capable of performing the husbandly act, even if they had to share him. Loss of a husband's virility is an issue she may be as responsible for as the feminising oestrogen which is now found in so much food and water.

Marriage on the basis of passion, wonder and admiration is considered the norm for many couples. You know better. If you have a choice between marriage and being either the toy boy or the sugar daddy, then you know the issue. The relationship is intended to be your launch pad into a new life after 60. Adventures come to an end. Therefore marriage is not really an option. Besides, you know that a biological self-based marriage is doomed to fail. So why risk all the trouble and expense of a divorce? The answer to that is down to an important decision. Are you going to be husband and turn the adventure of a relationship into a lifestyle, or are you going to embark on a series of toy boy marriages to gain money and possessions? Are you the sort of man who would pass for Don Juan on a bright day? In that case it is probable that you have little choice and a toy boy, unmarried relationship is your best bet. You then have the freedom to end it with your riches in the bank. But if you decide to remain with your partner whatever the outcome, then you are in the company of very many retired people who have turned what started out to be an adventure into a lifestyle.

Typical among this group are the retired Mediterranean sailors of both sexes and all ages from mid-fifties onwards who, having taken to the water, find that the biological demand for new horizons keeps them sailing around the Mediterranean in ever-decreasing circles. What starts out as a visit to every country ends as being constant short hops between islands or adjacent villages. The enthusiasm has gone and the adventure is now a way of life. Compensation for the other three selves comes in the form of reading or becoming a sort of 'Mr. Fix-it' for yacht owners. Not a lot different, in fact, to the life one leads on retirement without any future except pottering and wife-following. Books are the only release, because by second-hand means you can have as many in-the-head adventures as you wish. Every yacht has an abundance of books which do the rounds of the yachts. After reading you can recount the adventures to each other and feel part of a community. That is all that people with no common background or interests are able to do. Sad, is it not?

Now you see the pitfalls you will be better able to ensure that your adventure does not become a lifestyle. This is done quite simply by giving it a time limit. During your adventure it is important to be able to be on one's own. Company of friends or family may be included within the adventure, but the most important thing is solitude.

Why, you ask? Because solitude is the time you can hear your selves talking.

5

Self-Assessment

After a lifetime of work and constantly being surrounded by people and noise, you have probably had little chance to hear your selves. However, in any situation they are communicating. If you are involved in a one-self activity, such as the cognitive self during an arithmetic calculation, you may well find that it is you the person that you hear. You the person are merely monitoring the self. If you think back to a time when you last did calculations, you will see what I mean. I call the conscious that monitors the other consciouses the 'Executive Conscious'.

Now during your life you may have been aware of people dying who were younger than yourself or close to your age. Discounting people with physical illness, it seems a mystery why these people died. One of the clear indications is that they were dedicated people, often in the field of music, academia, art or literature. It seemed they had everything, yet their lives were wracked with depression, ending with their early demise. Clearly from the viewpoint of Reality Differential Analysis their ZOE was maintaining its state of equanimity by using principally one self. The fact that you are now retired means that your ZOE did not have quite the same struggle. You still might have had periods of depression, but you escaped the killing effect.

During your periods of solitude as you listen to your voices you will gain the chance to learn about yourself, which voice is dominant and whether it should be. You will find that you will begin to recognise each self from the language it uses. This whole process will take some time, perhaps as long as 40 days and nights! At the end of it you will have a much better idea of your person and how you need to change in order to have your ZOE receiving RDFs in all domains

You might be quite alarmed to realise that you operated your life using only the social and cognitive. Your psyche self was totally suppressed and your biological self compensated for its lack of physical contact and love by overeating. Its energies were turned to supporting the other two selves. You were known as a dedicated, hardworking employee, but your ZOE was kept stable only by the most delicate of manipulations. If you overate or drank too much, then unconsciously it was to ensure some high RDFs in the morning, when you had a hangover and stomach pains.

So now you know your problem. How can it be resolved? The basis for a happy state is a balanced ZOE with each domain contributing to elation. Your biological domain is a mess. Your biological self has practically single-handedly been creating high and low RDFs in order to maintain some sort of undulation of the ZOE. The two active domains have had a dominant role in your life, but their occupation with the world of employment and society has not made them positive creators of ZOE undulations. They have for many years been on a mission of survival with their responses due to the two selves endeavouring to make life bearable in a job that demanded nothing from the biological self.

You recall an occasion where a colleague was so taken with his secretary's see-through blouse and the beauty of her breasts peeking through her lacy brassiere that he forgot the cardinal role of the office. Do not stare. He found that instead of taking furtive glances at the display, he started to become obsessed. One day he touched his secretary's arm with his hand. That was almost forgivable and usually involved a whispering, "Oh, I'm sorry Miss Brown. I thought I was touching your chair back". But on this occasion his eyes were riveted to one of her nipples, which was protruding through a gap in the lace underwear, and he failed to speak or remove his hand from her arm. Worse still, his eyes were out like organ-stops as he drooled over her breasts. He did not even hear her speak to him.

However he heard Miss Hackett, the office manager, when she said, "Mr. Smith please come to my office". She immediately accused him of sexual harassment and he was sacked on the spot. His secretary was promoted to his job by way of compensation.

So your time at work has been a survival operation as you attempted to maintain your ZOE undulating state. This you found exhausting, resulting in flopping down in a chair at home and eating too much. Now all that is past. On this adventure you are going to lose weight, as you do not need to carry it around for the next 40 years or so. In the process you will learn from listening to your selves what your person needs.

Proper assessment is quite complex, but you will be able to get a firm idea of what is required after this section. Each domain must be looked at in turn and analysed. Some events, activities, thoughts and reactions will give high RDFs and some will give low. What you need to do is mentally assess all those things in that domain and decide whether they are good or bad (as a simple label) to your domain self. Then you tot up the good things and the bad things and come to a decision about the overall effect.

I would have four sheets of paper listing high and low RDF themes and then make an assessment from 1 to 10. I would also make an assessment of your ZOE width. What you are going to do will give you a crude pointer to whether you are gaining RDFs towards elation or depression and figuring an outcome.

The biological domain

The Biological Domain is your primary contact domain with the external world. For low RDFs you need adequate food and warmth, fresh air, trees and flowers, birds and other animals, sunlight, a feeling of being nurtured, activity and good health, a healthy sex life and other things you may already have thought of. High RDFs are not just the negation of the above. In their own way they have to be positively the opposite. For instance, not having a meal will not give you a high RDF, while being really hungry because you lost your food in a river whilst on a camping trip will give you a high RDF. Not being able to touch an animal for some reason will give high RDFs. Being away from your dog for an afternoon, will not. The real analysis is to listen to the biological self and decide, with the executive conscious, whether what is under issue is high or low. The agent of the domain is the biological self.

The Social Domain

The Social Domain is the learnt domain; what you did as a child in the social world to gain low RDFs may not be working for you in the present situation. Because the social domain and its agent, the social self, are functioning under some learnt rules they will be unaware of the consequences to others as they pursue low RDFs.

On retiring you may suddenly realise that something is wrong. The issues that give high or low RDFs are not as clear-cut as those for the biological self. For instance, your car is a status symbol which gives you low RDFs. It can also be a source of high RDFs in a traffic jam as your status is brought to the same level as the rest of the drivers. This is lessened by application of the 'Pyramid of Abuse' which is outlined in my book on happiness.

Your house is a great status symbol and gives low RDFs. However these are reduced by the ordinariness of your house compared to all the others in the locality. To counteract this reduction in low RDFs, you were constantly embarking on improvement operations to look different from the neighbours. On balance, providing you could keep one step ahead of your neighbours, you would gain low RDFs.

So you now consider the following; your job (or retirement role), your wife's job, the school your children go to (or went to), your education, your ability to play games with your neighbours and so on. Eventually you will decide when and if your social world contributes to your ZOE state of elation - or depresses it.

The Cognitive Domain

This is the domain which has advanced technology and put men on the Moon. At a lower level it is the domain which works out the family budget or decides how to get a piece of furniture through a doorway. This part of your self will have been used within the prescribed limits at work until eventually what was once a thinking process became a habit. This self has probably been a victim of circumstances and a source of high RDFs. Those plans at work which would have achieved so much were disregarded.

The difference between the thwarted attempt to park your car and the rejection of weeks of work is twofold. Parking is short-term and of the social domain, while your plans were over a long period and belong to your cognitive domain. Your cognitive self spent hours, days, even weeks, being frustrated at every turn. The whole process caused incredible stress and contributed to your biological self compensating by over-eating and drinking. Now that you have retired, dejected by your efforts being rejected, you have to find an executive role for your cognitive self.

An adventure, but not the one with a new wife or mistress, has to include decision-making of a technical nature which will not be frustrated by the actions of others. That is not to say that everyone will agree with you.

One of the groups of people who live for a long time

is the politicians. The level is important; immersing your cognitive self in political considerations involves the predictable and the unpredictable. These represent cognitive issues and problems which need to be resolved at each stage. Nothing is that simple. A good way to look at politics is to consider it as meteorology. Trying to get the right answer at a time and place affects every other place, and in turn the places affect your problem's solution as they too play their part. Both meteorology and politics represent a cognitive challenge of immense complexity.

Another challenge is academia. I know of people who have launched themselves into academic studies on retirement. Some who are now in their 80s have more degrees than their tutors and present their tutors with cognitive challenges as complex as the ones they are trying to resolve. Some men turn to engineering and create things from lumps of steel and brass. This of course involves the biological self as creator and the cognitive self as engineer. So you need to take a good hard look at your present cognitive self's role in life and try to satisfy its needs.

The Psyche Domain

The final self to consider is the psyche self. I originally called this domain the psychodynamic domain because at the time it seemed right. However, the notion of a psychodynamic self was not something I could accept. Since those early days in Reality Differential Theory, it has become apparent that each self has its own unconscious and that these are in communication with each other resolving the meaning of inputs. As each self has a different interpretation of what its input mean in self terms, it is not at all surprising, when the executive conscious has a view of the unconscious of all selves, that the impression its gets is one of confusion and chaos. The unconscious of the psyche self is like all the others, hidden from the conscious. Indeed, because of the demands of the cognitive and social selves, the psyche self has had little chance to make its presence felt to the executive, being a fundamental self which is peculiar to higher life forms. Its presence is often felt through the biological self when, for instance, a person enters an old church. An air of peace or tranquillity accompanies the person round the church and when they leave there is a sense of loss as the world of noise and clamour hits them.

To enable the psyche self to pervade the person and become known to the executive, certain conditions must be met. The first of these is silence. During this phase you will become aware of the noisiness of the selves. However, one of these selves is generating peace and tranquillity which has a sound of its own. This is the psyche self. The second condition is solitude. This is not the same as being on your own. Solitude is when the silence around you starts to communicate with your unconscious and conscious. You will develop a strange feeling of not being in solitude, as you allow the place you have chosen to work its magic. Such places as woods, forests, mountains, the sea, deserts and the world of ice and snow will all work to release the unconscious to the individual.

Now in the world of jobs and people, you may have thought that you had no contact with the psyche self. You would be wrong. In the still of the night when your other three unconscious selves are trying to resolve the problems and hurts of the day, it is the psyche's unconscious which casts peace on the proceedings so that you awake feeling at peace with the world.

The problem with psychology is that nothing can be proved in the physical sense. We use terms like 'intuition' to explain the executive's awareness of an unconscious happening. This is frequently put forward as a feminine trait. The truth is of course that both men and women have the facility of consciously registering urgent information from the unconscious. Interestingly, people with a claim to be spiritual or psychic or to be able to see into the future have an abundance of intuitions or 'messages'. It is likely therefore, that modern life with all its distractions is the reason why you have not been blessed with these gifts.

Because the psyche self is not something we can judge or be rational about, it represents a part of us that is a little frightening. As with the other selves the domain has the power to control the ZOE to the exclusion of all the others. Young people sucked into an organisation aimed at exploiting the psyche self have discovered that there is a point at which people have a choice, between a life with three selves or a much simpler life with one. Such a life would be different and possibly tranquil. However, the ZOE requires inputs from all its selves to create undulated domains, leading to the whole ZOE shifting and undulating.

I have spent some time on the psyche domain because it represents more of an unknown than the others. Because of this, you might be tempted to sell up everything and move into a monastery. Had this been the right thing to do for you then you would have done it as a young man. Once you have found that source of peace, which might have been during an adventure, you will be able to call upon it more and more as you grow older and the physical world ceases to mean so much.

Assessing the needs of each self is not as simple as you might have first thought. Each has its own offerings and requirements from you. Just being aware of your ZOE and ensuring that it has an input of RDFs to its benefit, so that it maintains width and undulation, is something many who are lost in a world of confusion would be grateful to accomplish.

6

Adventure –
The Challenge

So life begins at sixty?

As 60 approaches you may have been fortunate enough to have wound down your daily grind to less than 40 hours a week. If you are, for instance, a school teacher, the normal day ends with marking books or some other task necessary for you to do your job. The resulting week for many teachers is well over 40 hours, with many doing around 10 hours a day. Stress and exhaustion levels are high and generally one does not have the time or energy to work out how the week could be made easier. The solution, of course, is to rethink your week's work during the holidays. After a suitable period of rest a way may be found to reduce your workload.

I want you to assume that those years leading up to sixty, irrespective of your work, saw a reduction in workload and hours. You will have been aware of Parkinson's Law and the Peter Principle, both of which are mentioned in my book 'The Pursuit of Happiness'. From this book you may have found out about the things which made you unhappy, made you work long hours and continually worked at home in the evenings.

So at sixty you now have the energy and motivation for an Adventure. What you may decide to do, from driving a motorhome around the world to creating a simple business involving one of your hobbies, will depend on your personality.

Let me tell you what I did.

First of all I found out what sort of person I was, and that was Biological-Cognitive. Whilst I could be sociable on occasions, being social was not much of my personal being. My psyche self was triggered off when I was up a mountain looking at the view, or listening to music and certain singers. I have a liking for water, so the logical thing for me was sailing somewhere and taking music with me.

The first thing to decide was, where? I decided to do something different, so I looked on the internet to find out where people sailed and how many had sailed to any particular place. I found that most trips of note had been across the Atlantic. A much smaller number had sailed round the world, but both trips had become commonplace adventures. My mind drifted to the untried, the failed and the impossible.

I ended up thinking of the Arctic, but what to do? Captain Cook had tried to find the North West Passage in 1778, but had found so much ice that he turned south to avoid being caught in the ice for a winter in the Bering Strait. In 1845 Sir John Franklin, with the rank of Captain, attempted his voyage from the Atlantic side. Nothing more was heard of him and it was assumed that he was slowly making his way through the passage. In 2014 the wreck of his ship was discovered in relatively shallow water. An odd thing about the Franklin expedition was the promotion of Captain Franklin to the rank of Rear Admiral in 1852. They had only had enough food for three years, so he must long since have died.

So, the North West Passage had been attempted by large ships and seemed an impossible dream for anyone in a small vessel. I spent weeks studying the ice conditions of the Arctic to find out for myself what might be possible and maybe not tried before. The first thing that became apparent was that Arctic ice melted differently each summer, and at some time each year vast sections of the seas were free of ice, or to be more accurate, had less than 10% covering the sea.

I decided to try what seemed impossible, given that I needed 80% luck. The dream was to sail eastwards across the top of Russia and Canada. This had not been done before in any one year, although the North East passage across Russia had been done, as had the North West passage, by different groups and in a different year.

So, at 60, I decided to circumnavigate the North Pole in one season. I started to plan the trip and slowly built up my stock of Arctic clothing. As 64 approached my mind turned to the type of craft for the voyage. I studied write-ups and visited many boatyards to see firsthand if I liked the size, strength and layout of any particular craft.

In late 2003, at 64, I discovered a tough little craft with a class history of voyages all over the globe. I purchased *Mohican*, a 30-foot Seadog ketch. A surveyor's opinion was this class of hull was a 100-year hull. That winter and early spring she was checked over and made ready for sea. In April of 2004 I sailed for the Arctic from Ramsgate in Kent. I was single-handed, as apparently no one wanted to sail with me. My Arctic adventure had begun. As it is described in my book about my sailing trips I intend to give only a few highlights here. I got locked in the ice in the Barents Sea, north of Russia. A polar bear tried to join me by hanging onto the shrouds. I did not think it intended to join me as crew, so I sent it away. I developed engine trouble, with the engine overheating.

I was invited by the Russians to enter one of their ports for repairs. Before reaching the port *Mohican* was arrested and towed 200 nautical miles into Archangel. After a week I was towed 400 nautical miles to the border between Norway and Russia and then shadowed by a large warship until I was a long way from Russia. I was removed from Russia because as I was single-handed, the Russians took the view that I must be a spy. I returned to the UK.

In late May 2006 I sailed for the Arctic. The Russians in Murmansk gave me written permission to sail the North East Passage across Russia. After a month of waiting for the 'go' I received an instruction for me to go to Norway as they had changed their minds; another adventure curtailed!

This time I decided to salvage the trip by sailing to Svalbard. In Longyearbyen, Capital of Svalbard, I decided to sail up the west coast of Spitsbergen and continue until I reached the ice cap. This I did, getting stuck in the ice for a day. I returned south via the east coast of Spitsbergen, being chased by icebergs and dodging large sheets of invisible ice. After that circumnavigation I sailed south until I reached the Orkney Islands, which I approached without a chart. As

I entered the islands my steering wheel decided to break off from the shaft.

One lifeboat and fishing boat later I was in Kirkwall, being propositioned by a 14-year-old girl who said she was 18. Later in the year I returned to Ramsgate. By now I had become a celebrated failure of Kent. Despite the fame, I found that my hunger for adventure had declined.

In 2008 I sold my house and moved into a rented property. In 2011 I sailed for the Arctic again. I lost my roller-reefing forestay and genoa sail off the coast of Norway, 30 miles off the entrance to Bergen. I decided to discontinue my Arctic attempt and so turned my trip into a simple cruise, returning to Ramsgate in September after visiting Bergen, the Shetland Islands and Lowestoft.

Later in the year I discovered a boat which needed rigging but was ideal for a trip to the Arctic. It was of heavy steel construction and 43 feet long. I had the vessel rigged and fitted out. All I needed was a crew. Now who did I know who might fancy a long sailing trip into the Arctic?

Well, May 2012 saw me sailing *Mohican Too* to the Arctic on my own, yet again! The trip was interesting. I eventually reached Vadso, north-east Norway, in the late summer and found a good mooring. Still no crew, but a Swedish lady expressed an interest. I found I had a crew of one. In June 2013 she joined me, with another Swedish lady. I now had a crew of two. We sailed for Murmansk.

The pirates of Murmansk would not let us leave until they had around $2000 from us. I did not pay, but after 19 days we were released and forbidden to go across Russia. We were shadowed by radar to make sure that we went to Norway. They were in radio contact all the time. "We know where you are" they kept telling us.

That year the ice did not clear, so it would have been impossible to make a circumnavigation around the pole.

We decided to make our trip into a cruise and went to Svalbard, Greenland, Iceland, the Faroe Islands, the Shetland Islands, Orkney, Heligoland, the Kiel Canal and then across the Baltic Sea.

In Greenland we were not allowed to leave by the local pirates until we had paid $3500. Later in the East

Baltic Sea we were run down by a Russian nuclear materials carrier which removed our mast and caused an inflow of sea water.

Well, that is the bones of the big Adventure. More followed, ending at Uddevalla, Sweden in 2014 when I was 75.

Having now married one of the Swedish crew and written about my adventures, I realise that I am now on a new adventure and as the boat is conveniently at hand in Uddevalla I am planning another trip.

Your Adventure

Before planning your own adventure, you must first work out what sort of person you are. Then you should be aware that your normal way of life must be changed. If for instance you think the idea of sailing, climbing or travelling is foolhardy, stupid or just plain crazy, then you may want a more cognitive challenge. Perhaps you will design a new car, write a book, build a house extension or lock yourself away in a room eight hours a day designing an antigravity unit, or capturing the sound of long-ago broadcasts. Whatever you decide to do, good luck!

Remember, success is actually starting the adventure with a goal in mind. You cannot fail, even if your goal has to be changed. People may laugh and scoff. Only you will know the hardships and the challenges you have overcome to be where you are, and that is all that matters.

www.ingramcontent.com/pod-product-compliance
Lightning Source LLC
Chambersburg PA
CBHW070116070426
42448CB00040B/3049